Mason Jar Meals

Surprisingly Quick, Easy and Healthy Mason Jar Meal Recipe Ideas for People on the Go

By Jessica Jacobs

© **Copyright 2014 - All rights reserved.**

In no way is it legal to reproduce, duplicate, or transmit any part of this document in either electronic means or in printed format. Recording of this publication is strictly prohibited and any storage of this document is not allowed unless with written permission from the publisher. All rights reserved.

The information provided herein is stated to be truthful and consistent, in that any liability, in terms of inattention or otherwise, by any usage or abuse of any policies, processes, or directions contained within is the solitary and utter responsibility of the recipient reader. Under no circumstances will any legal responsibility or blame be held against the publisher for any reparation, damages, or monetary loss due to the information herein, either directly or indirectly.

Respective authors own all copyrights not held by the publisher.

Legal Notice:

This eBook is copyright protected. This is only for personal use. You cannot amend, distribute, sell, use, quote or paraphrase any part or the content within this eBook without the consent of the author or copyright owner. Legal action will be pursued if this is breached

Disclaimer Notice

Please note the information contained within this document is for educational and entertainment purposes only. Every attempt has been made to provide accurate, up to date and reliable complete information. No warranties of any kind are expressed or implied. Readers acknowledge that the author is not engaging in the rendering of legal, financial or professional advice.

By reading this document, the reader agrees that under no circumstances are we responsible for any losses, direct or indirect, which are incurred as a result of the use of information contained within this document, including, but not limited to, —errors, omissions, or inaccuracies.

Introduction

Canning and food preservation has been going on for ages. Earlier, canning was done in a glass jar and it was covered with a flat tin lid, which was sealed with wax. These jars were messy and were not reusable.

Decades later, Mason Jars became popular, due to their reusable properties. John Landis Mason invented these jars in 1858. He was a tinsmith by profession based in New York City. He used reusable molded glass jars to preserve food. He invented a machine by which threads were cut on to the lid, which could be screwed on to the jar.

The lids he used were made of zinc with a rubber ring. The rubber produced the seal and the lids maintained it. Because of the vacuum created in the jar, food remains fresh and intact without any bacterial growth inside the jar.

Mason jars are affordable, reusable, convenient, appealing to the eye and easy to use. Storing and carrying meals in Mason jar is just the thing for you when you have shortage of time. If you prepare and store your meals in advance, all you need to do is grab a filled jar, pick a spoon and take them with you on your journey and you can have fresh, nutritious, homemade meals all the time, no matter how hectic your life is.

Not just that, Mason jar recipes make excellent personalized gifts for your dear ones. With the holiday season coming up, you don't have to scratch your head on gifting options. From salads to desserts, in this eBook we demonstrate the ways to make all kinds of quick, delicious and healthy Mason jar recipes.

Most ingredients that have been mentioned here are easily available in your kitchen. So, without much ado, let us begin this magical journey of learning Mason Jar Recipes.

About This Book

You will find over 30 recipes that would help you enjoy making healthy mason jar meals.

These mason jar recipes are grouped into seven sections.

First section talks about breakfast recipes.

Second section is about different salad mason jar recipes.

Third section tackles lunch and dinner meals.

Fourth section is where you will find a variety of soup recipes for the mason jar.

Fifth section is where dessert recipes in mason jars are shared.

Sixth section surprises you with smoothies in a jar recipes.

And lastly the seventh section discusses beverages in a jar.

This book has a variety of mason jar recipes that would inspire you to cook and eat healthy meals even if you are always on the go. You can check out the comprehensive Table of Contents for the recipes included in this book.

At the end of the book, you can find concluding remarks and key takeaways with recommended websites and books for further readings.

Table of Contents

Chapter 1: Breakfast Recipes for Mason Jar   1

  Yogurt and Fruit Parfait   2

  Mason jar Granola Parfait   3

  Overnight Oatmeal Breakfast in Different Delicious Flavors   5

  Eggs and Bacon in Mason Jar   7

  Blueberry and Grilled Peach Quinoa Parfaits   8

  Cherry Chia Jam Overnight Oats   10

  Cherry Chia Jam   11

  Mason Jar Breakfast Casserole   12

  Toasted Oat and Coconut Muesli   14

  Maple Fried Apples   16

  Cottage Cheese & Yogurt Parfait   18

Chapter 2: Salads in a Mason Jar   19

  Apple Salad with Berries   20

  Chicken and Bean Salad   21

  Chick Peas Salad   23

  Pasta Salad   25

  Burritos in a Jar   26

  Salad with Orange Ginger Dressing   27

  Fresh Mozzarella and Spinach Salad   29

  Spinach, Blueberry, and Blue Cheese Salad   30

  Artichoke and Tortellini Salad   31

  Stone fruit and Fava bean Salad   32

Chapter 3: Lunch/Dinner in a Mason Jar — 34

- Zucchini Rice — 35
- Roasted Sweet Potato with Quinoa — 37
- Shrimp, Bacon and Feta Cheese delight — 39
- Californian rolls in a jar — 41
- Pepperoni Spaghetti — 43
- Mason Jar Chicken Cordon Bleu — 44
- Rice and Bean Burrito — 46
- Mason Jar Stromboli — 48
- Chicken Curry with Cilantro Rice — 50

Chapter 4: Soups in a Jar — 52

- Tortilla Soup — 53
- Vegetable Soup — 55
- Chicken Noodle Soup — 56
- Pasta Soup — 58
- Instant Noodle Soup in a Jar — 60
- Beef Barley Soup Mix in a Jar — 62
- Layered Dried Bean Soup Mix — 64
- Rainbow Bean Soup Mix — 66
- Meat and Tomato Mix soup — 68
- Holiday Split Pea Soup Mix — 70

Chapter 5: Desserts in a Mason Jar — 72

- Banana and cream — 73
- Caramel Brownies — 75
- Fruit Parfait — 76
- Blueberry Cheesecake — 78

Butterfinger pies in a jar	81
Buttermilk Panna Cotta	83
Molten orange chocolate lava cakes	84
Creme Caramel	86
Salted Caramel Brownie Trifles	88
Banana Split Parfait	90
Chapter 6: Smoothies in a Jar	92
Fruity Green tea smoothie	93
Banana Smoothie	94
Strawberry Almond Butter Smoothie	95
Mango Smoothie	96
Banana and Peanut Butter Smoothie	97
Strawberry Oatmeal Smoothie	98
Quick & Easy Mason Jar Smoothie	99
Make Ahead Smoothies	100
Chapter 7: Beverages in a Mason Jar	101
White Chocolate Latte	102
Lemonade	103
Fruit Delight	104
Coffee in a jar	106
Chocó-coffee delight	107
Strawberry Milk	108
Hot spiced tea and cider mix	109
Blueberry Infused Vodka Lemonade	110
Iced Mocha	111
Conclusion	112

Key Takeaways From This Book	113
How To Put This Information Into Action	114
RESOURCES FOR FURTHER VIEWING AND READING	115
PREVIEW OF HYDROGEN PEROXIDE HANDBOOK	116
Did You Like Mason Jar Meals Surprisingly Quick, Easy and Healthy Mason Jar Meal Recipe Ideas for People on the Go?	122
More Books You Might Like	124

Chapter 1: Breakfast Recipes for Mason Jar

Yogurt and Fruit Parfait

Serves 2

Ingredients:

- 2 cups plain Greek yogurt, unflavored
- 2/3 cup oats, uncooked
- 2 teaspoons chia seeds (optional)
- 4 tablespoons milk
- 2 cups mixed fruit of your choice
- ¼ cup berries
- 2 tablespoons nuts of your choice

Method:

1. In a bowl, mix yogurt, oats, chia seeds and milk.
2. Fill half of this mix in Mason jars.
3. Layer with half the portion of fruits, berries and nuts.
4. The next layer is the yogurt mixture.
5. Finally layer with the remaining fruits, berries and nuts.
6. Tightly screw on the lids.
7. Refrigerate overnight.
8. It can store up to 3 days.

Mason jar Granola Parfait

Serves 3

Ingredients:

- 2 cups plain yogurt, unflavored and low fat
- 2 cups fruits or berries of your choice
- ¼ cup honey
- ¾ cup rolled oats
- ¼ cup nuts, chopped and seeds of your choice
- ½ tablespoon olive oil
- ½ teaspoon cinnamon
- ¼ teaspoon vanilla extract
- A pinch of salt

Method:

1. Preheat the oven to 325 degrees.
2. Meanwhile, in a large bowl mix together the oats, nuts, olive oil, cinnamon, vanilla, salt and ½ of the honey.
3. Spread evenly on a greased baking dish.
4. Bake for around 45 minutes, stirring it every 15 minutes.

5. The granola should be golden brown if not then bake further for another 10-15 minutes.

6. To assemble in the mason jars, first fill in the yogurt then pour the remaining honey over it.

7. Next layer it with fruits and then granola.

8. Repeat the layer.

9. Tightly screw on the lids and refrigerate.

10. It can store up to 3 days.

Overnight Oatmeal Breakfast in Different Delicious Flavors

Serves 4

Ingredients:

- 3 Cups almond milk/ skimmed milk/coconut milk
- ½ cup yogurt, strained
- 1 cup rolled oats

Variations

- 1 cup Pumpkin puree, a pinch each of cinnamon, nutmeg and ginger
- 1 cup Fresh mango or strawberries finely chopped or blended with 2 tablespoons honey
- 1 cup peeled and chopped apples and a pinch of cinnamon powder
- 3 teaspoons espresso coffee powder and 4 teaspoons brown sugar topped with cherries and toasted almonds or hazelnuts
- 3 tablespoons peanut butter. Layer with sliced bananas
- ½ cup grated carrots, ½ cup chopped pineapple, 3 tablespoons chopped walnuts, 3 tablespoons maple syrup and ½ teaspoon cinnamon powder.
- 1 cup fresh blackberries, 3 tablespoons toasted and slivered almonds, 1 tablespoon crystallized ginger

- 3-4 Bananas sliced and 2 tablespoons cocoa powder
- 1 cup blueberries, ¼ teaspoon almond extract, ¼ teaspoon cinnamon powder
- 4 teaspoons maple syrup, pinch of salt, 2 teaspoons shredded coconut and 1 tablespoon slivered almonds. In this recipe use coconut milk.

Method:

1. Mix all the ingredients in a large bowl.
2. Put a layer of it in the mason jar.
3. Layer with your choice of variation.
4. Repeat the layer.
5. If you don't like layered, then mix together all the ingredients and store in the mason jars.
6. Tightly screw on the lids.
7. Refrigerate overnight.
8. It can store up to 3 days.

Eggs and Bacon in Mason Jar

Serves 2

Ingredients:

- 4 eggs

- 1 cup spinach, finely shredded

- ½ cup cheese, shredded (if you love cheese, you can increase the quantity as per taste)

- 1 cup bacon, crumbled

- Salt and pepper as per your taste

Method:

1. In a large bowl, mix together the eggs, spinach, cheese, salt and pepper.

2. Fill in mason jar.

3. Microwave for 1 ½ to 2 minutes. Check it in between.

4. As it is being micro waved, the egg will rise to the top of the jar. Do not worry.

5. Top with bacon and extra cheese if you desire.

6. Tightly screw the lids.

7. Store in the refrigerator.

Blueberry and Grilled Peach Quinoa Parfaits

Serves 4

Ingredients:

- 4 teaspoons pecans, chopped
- 4 teaspoons honey, agave or maple syrup
- 2 containers or 1 cup vanilla Greek yogurt
- 1 cup blueberries
- 1 cup quinoa, cooked and cooled
- 2 halved peaches, pit removed

Method:

1. Preheat the grill to medium and then put both halves of the peach onto the grill. With the cut side facing down, heat for about 4-5 minutes, and then flip it over for an additional 4-5 minutes. When ready, the peach should have caramelized and juicy. Another option is to roast the peach halves in a preheated oven at 425 degrees F, cut side facing up. Bake on a baking sheet for about 20-35 minutes until tender.

2. Take it from the grill and now position it in the fridge to cool. Now remove the peels and chop your peach into ½-inch slices.

3. Into the bottom of each of 4 jars, put 2 teaspoons of quinoa. Add in 2 tablespoons of blueberries as a topping, 2 teaspoons of yoghurt, about 1/8th of the

peaches, ½ teaspoon of pecans, and a ½ teaspoon of maple syrup.

4. Do it again for the layers, and use the reserved peach slice as a topping. You may also garnish with a few blueberries if preferred.

Cherry Chia Jam Overnight Oats

Serves 3-4

Ingredients:

- Chopped cherries and almonds, for garnish
- 2 tablespoons cocoa nibs
- ½ teaspoon cinnamon, ground
- 2 teaspoons pure vanilla extract
- 2 tablespoons pure maple syrup
- 2 tablespoons chia seeds
- 1½ cups almond milk or nut milk, unsweetened
- 1 cup rolled oats, gluten-free
- 1 recipe chia cherry jam (see below)

Method:

1. Into an airtight container, add in cocoa nibs, cinnamon, vanilla extract, maple syrup, chia seeds, almond milk and rolled oats. Whisk the mixture gently, and then put under refrigeration for 8 hours, or overnight.
2. Layer the cherry chia jam and the oats into about 3-4 jars. If preferred, you can use chopped almonds or cherries to garnish. Serve or put into your fridge.

Cherry Chia Jam

Ingredients:

- 3 tablespoons chia seeds
- 1 tablespoon pure maple syrup
- 2 cups sweet cherries, pitted and de-stemmed

Method:

1. Add the maple syrup and cherries to a blender and blend on high for about two minutes or until smooth.
2. Pour this into an airtight container then stir in chia seeds. Cover and put in the fridge for at least four hours.

Mason Jar Breakfast Casserole

Serves 2

Ingredients:

- ¼ teaspoon pepper
- ½ teaspoon sea salt
- ½ teaspoon nutmeg
- ¼ cup coconut milk
- 6 eggs, beaten
- 1 candy onion, shredded
- 1 small sweet potato, peeled and shredded
- 2 sweet Italian sausage links
- 1 teaspoon bacon fat or ghee

Method:

1. Preheat your oven to 375 degrees F as you grease two 16-ounce Mason jars using bacon fat. Into a large skillet, melt some bacon fat over medium-heat and then break apart the brown sausage in the skillet.

2. Beat the eggs with salt and pepper, nutmeg and coconut milk, and then stir in the onion, shredded sweet potato and the browned sausage.

3. Add all these contents into the mason jars.

4. Into a 9x9 inch baking dish, prepare a water bath for the Mason jars and allow the water to sit about ½ inch high on the mason jars. Now bake for about 40-50 minutes, to have the insides of the casserole set. When done, remove the jars from heat and allow to chill for 2 minutes.

5. You can as well use 4-8 ounce Mason jars to cook faster in 20-25 minutes.

Toasted Oat and Coconut Muesli

Serves 4

Ingredients:

- ½ teaspoon nutmeg, freshly grated
- ¼ teaspoon salt
- ¼ cup chia seeds
- 1 cup candied ginger, coarsely chopped
- 1 cup dried cranberries
- ½ teaspoon cinnamon, ground
- 1 cup dry roasted almonds, coarsely chopped
- 1 cup coconut flakes, unsweetened
- 4 cups old-fashioned oats

To Serve:

- Pure maple syrup
- Cold almond milk
- Frozen blueberries

Method:

1. Into the center and the upper end of the oven, put 2 racks and then preheat the oven to 350 degrees F. Into unlined and ungreased baking sheet, place the oats and

put the coconut into another baking sheet that is unlined and unbaked.

2. Toast the coconut and the oats for about 5-7 minutes, until coconut turns fragrant and golden brown. Pay close attention to the coconut since it browns quickly. Now remove the coconut and oats from your oven and allow to cool.

3. Toss together chia seeds, oats, salt, dried cranberries, spices and coconut in a large bowl and then store into Mason jars. You should prepare the muesli a few hours before serving, or the night before serving.

4. To serve, use a good amount of muesli scooping into a bowl. Use frozen berries to top, pour the almond milk over the blueberries and muesli to cover the berries. Cover and keep under refrigeration overnight. To serve, drizzle with maple syrup and enjoy.

Maple Fried Apples

Serves 7

Ingredients:

For Maple Fried Apples:

- 1 teaspoon cinnamon
- 1 tablespoon brown sugar
- ½ cup maple syrup
- ½ teaspoon kosher salt
- 6 Granny Smith apples
- ½ stick butter

For Pigs in a Blanket Pancakes:

- 14 breakfast sausage links
- 4 tablespoons butter, melted
- 2 eggs
- 1½ cups milk
- 2 tablespoons sugar
- 4 teaspoons baking powder
- ½ teaspoon kosher salt
- 2 cups flour

Method:

1. To prepare the apples, melt some butter over medium heat in a large skillet. Add in the other ingredients and cook until tender and the liquid is absorbed. This should take about 30 minutes.

2. Start to prepare the pancakes, as the pancakes get ready. First, preheat your oven to 350 degrees F as you grease 7 (8-ounce) mason jars of capacity, set aside.

3. Whisk together the dry ingredients in a bowl, and whisk eggs and milk in a separate bowl. Pour the egg mixture over the dry ingredients and stir well to combine. Add in butter.

4. Sub-divide the butter between 7 jars and put about 4 ounces into each Mason jar. Into each jar, push 2 sausage links and then put the jars onto a sturdy jellyroll pan. Now bake the contents of the jar until a toothpick inserted into the cake comes out clean, for about 17 minutes.

5. Remove the baked cakes from your oven and then run a knife around each of the cake. Then dump out onto a plate, before slicing each into 5 medallions. You can serve with maple syrup or Maple Fried Apples as per your preference.

Cottage Cheese & Yogurt Parfait

Serves 4-6

Ingredients:

- 1 cup granola
- 1 cup vanilla yogurt
- 2 cups cottage cheese
- 1 tablespoon maple syrup
- 1 cup fruit, fresh or frozen

Method:

1. Start by tossing maple syrup and fruit to coat and then set aside. Into a bowl, combine yoghurt and cottage cheese and then sub-divide the mixture into 4 Mason jars.

2. Use the fruit mixture to evenly top, ensuring that the juices from the mixture collects at the bottom of the jar.

3. Use granola to sprinkle onto the mixture, and refrigerate until ready to be used, or serve immediately. Be aware that your granola would begin to soften as it chills.

Chapter 2:
Salads in a Mason Jar

Apple Salad with Berries

Serves 2

Ingredients:

- 2 cups apple, chopped
- 1 cup wheat berries, boiled
- 1 cup of berries (black berry or blue berries or cranberries) fresh or dried
- 1 onion, minced
- Parsley, chopped for garnishing
- 1 tablespoon olive oil
- 1 tablespoon balsamic vinegar
- 1 tablespoon lemon juice

Method:

1. To make the dressing: whisk the olive oil, lemon juice and balsamic vinegar
2. Mix rest of the ingredients in a large bowl.
3. Toss the dressing in the salad.
4. Fill up the mason jars.
5. Tightly screw the lids.
6. Store in refrigerator.
7. Can store up to 3 days.

Chicken and Bean Salad

Serves 2

Ingredients:

- 1 Whole chicken breast (grilled or poached)
- ½ cup black beans canned
- ½ cup corn, canned
- ½ cup tomatoes, diced
- ½ cup lettuce, chopped

For the dressing:

- 2 tablespoon plain Greek yogurt
- 1 ounce goat cheese, crumbled
- 2 tablespoons cilantro
- ½ lemon juice
- ½ avocado
- ¼ teaspoon cumin
- 2 tablespoons water

Method:

1. To make the dressing, puree all the ingredients of the dressing in a food processor.

2. Shred the grilled chicken into small pieces.

3. Construct the jar as follows:
   Bottom layer – avocado dressing
   Next layer – corn
   Next layer – beans
   Next layer – tomatoes
   Next layer – chicken
   Last layer – lettuce

4. Tightly screw the lids and refrigerate.

5. Toss it before eating.

Chick Peas Salad

Serves 4

Ingredients:

- 2 cups chick peas, boiled
- 1 cup tomatoes, chopped
- ½ cup spring onion, chopped
- ½ cup red onion, chopped
- 1 cup olives, chopped
- ½ cup piquillo peppers
- 1 cup fresh spinach, shredded
- 4 tablespoon lemon vinaigrette dressing
- Juice of 1 large lemon
- ½ cup olive oil
- Salt and pepper to taste

Method:

1. Construct the jar as follows:
   Bottom layer – dressing
   Next layer – chickpeas
   Next layer – tomatoes
   Next layer – spring onions
   Next layer – onions

    Next layer – piquillo peppers
    Last layer-- spinach

2. Tightly screw on the lids. Refrigerate

3. Toss the salad before eating

Pasta Salad

Serves 4

Ingredients:

- 2 cups rigatoni pasta, cooked al dente
- 1 cup cherry tomatoes
- 1 cup cucumber, chopped
- 1 cup feta cheese, crumbled
- ½ cup spinach, shredded
- ½ cup mint leaves
- ½ cup fresh basil leaves
- 4 tablespoons basil pesto

Method:

1. Take all the ingredients and mix them in a large bowl.
2. Fill in the mason jars.
3. Tightly screw the lids.
4. Refrigerate.
5. Can store up to 3 days.

Burritos in a Jar

Serves 2

Ingredients:

- 1/2 cup quinoa, cooked
- ¾ cup zesty black beans
- 2 cups lettuce, chopped
- ½ cup kale, de-ribbed, thinly chopped
- ½ cup sprouts
- 1 cup cherry tomato salsa
- 4 tablespoons Greek yogurt, plain
- 2 tablespoons salsa juice

Method:

1. Layer the jars as follows:
   Bottom layer – quinoa
   Next layer – zesty black beans
   Next layer – lettuce, followed by kale
   Next layer – cherry tomato salsa and salsa juice
   Next layer – Greek yogurt
   Top layer – sprouts

2. Tightly screw the lids on the jar. Refrigerate.

3. To serve, toss the salad.

Salad with Orange Ginger Dressing

Serves 4

Ingredients:

For the Salad:

- Kosher salt, to taste
- ½ cup fresh parsley, finely chopped
- 1 ½ cups green pepper, diced
- 1 ½ cups red pepper, diced
- 1 cup carrots, diced
- 1 cup edamame
- 1 cup quinoa, uncooked
- 1 cup wheat berries, uncooked

For the dressing:

- ¼ teaspoon kosher salt
- 1 tablespoon lime juice, fresh
- 1 tablespoon fresh ginger, minced
- 1 tablespoon apple cider vinegar
- 1/3 cup apple juice, 100 percent pure
- 2/3 cup orange juice, 100 percent pure

Method:

1. Add quinoa and 1 ½ cups of water into a medium-sized pot and bring to a boil. Minimize the heat to low and simmer when covered for about 15-20 minutes. Closely monitor this mixture to avoid burning.

2. Add 2 cups of water into a separate pot. Add the wheat berries and cook until chewy and tender. The mixture should cook for 5 minutes more compared to quinoa.

3. Chop the veggies and whisk together your dressing ingredients in a jar. Then set aside. Into each of your Mason jars, add in ¼ cup of edamame, 2 tablespoons of parsley, ¼ cup of carrots, ½ cup of quinoa, ¼ cup of red pepper and ¼ cup of wheat berries. Push it down a little, repeating as necessary.

4. You can as well mix the salad with the dressing in a big bowl. Keep refrigerated for about 5-6 days.

Fresh Mozzarella and Spinach Salad

Serves: 5

Ingredients:

- 10 cups baby spinach
- 2 cups dry pasta, whole grain, cooked
- 10 ounces fresh mozzarella
- 1 quart grape tomatoes
- 10 tablespoons balsamic vinegar dressing

Method:

1. Sub-divide your ingredients into 5 Mason jars starting with the dressing, followed by tomatoes, then mozzarella, pasta and finally the spinach. Put a lid onto the jar and then close tight.

2. To coat the dressing, shake the jar and then pour into a bowl and serve

Spinach, Blueberry, and Blue Cheese Salad

Serves 1

Ingredients:

- 3 tablespoons Red Wine Vinaigrette
- 2 ounces blue cheese, crumbled
- ¼ cup almonds, shaved or sliced
- 3 cups spinach leaves, divided
- ½ cup blueberries

Method:

1. Layer the blueberries at the bottom of the jar and then follow the next layer with 2 cups of spinach, then almonds and then the remaining cup of spinach. Finish the layering with the blue cheese.

2. Make a parchment paper cup on top of the blue cheese and then pour in the Red Wine Vinaigrette. Now seal the jar and put under refrigeration until ready to serve.

3. In case the salad is to be eaten immediately, you can keep the dressing in the bottom of the jar and then do away with the parchment paper cup.

Artichoke and Tortellini Salad

Serves: 5

Ingredients:

- 5 cups arugula blend salad /bagged spinach
- 1 quart cherry tomatoes, halved
- 5 ounces goat cheese
- 1 red onion, chopped
- 4 ounces of cooked dried cheese-filled tortellini
- 2 cans of quartered artichoke hearts
- 10 tablespoons Italian dressing

Method:

1. Layer each of 5-quart mason jars with your ingredients. Start with the dressing, then tomatoes, onions, then the artichokes, tortellini, the goat cheese and finally with the spinach or arugula blend.

2. To serve, shake the salad and then pour into bowl. You can also prepare the salads about 5 days ahead of time and then keep in the fridge.

Stone fruit and Fava bean Salad

Serves 1

Ingredients:

- 1 spring onion
- 1 ½ tablespoons virgin olive oil
- 1 lime, juice plus zest
- 1 small handful mint leaves
- Lime/Mint dressing

For Salad:

- Pinch of salt
- 1 clove garlic, minced
- 1 teaspoon virgin coconut oil
- 25 whole fava beans
- 2 cups leafy greens
- 1 nectarine, pitted and sliced
- 2 apricots, pitted and sliced
- ½ avocado, pitted and peeled
- ¼ cup pistachios: shelled, raw and unsalted
- 1 small cucumber, julienned

Method:

1. Start by rinsing, peeling and cutting the spring onions finely and then add in the onions and other ingredients to a pestle then grind using mortar until it's fully combined. Then pour into the bottom of the mason jar of choice.

2. To make the salad, separate the fava beans from their pod and then peel them from the green leathery skin.

3. Into a frying pan, heat coconut oil over medium heat, add in garlic and cook until it turns golden. Add in the fava beans, salt; and fry the mixture for 1-2 minutes. You want to eliminate the raw taste and then infuse the fava beans into garlic. Now set it aside.

4. Layer your Mason jar, starting with Julienne cucumber, followed by the fried fava beans, the stone fruits, crushed pistachios, and the greens. The stone fruits include avocado, nectarine, and apricots.

5. To serve, turn the Mason jar upside down onto your plate, with the leafy greens at the base to allow the dressing to infuse all the layers. You may also put the dressing in a little jar and pour it over your salad.

Chapter 3: Lunch/Dinner in a Mason Jar

Zucchini Rice

Serves 2

Ingredients:

- 1 ½ cup brown rice, cooked
- 2 small zucchinis, sliced lengthwise, grilled
- 1 yellow bell pepper, roasted, thinly sliced
- 1 red bell pepper, roasted, thinly sliced
- ½ cup carrot, shredded
- 4 tablespoons cashews, whole
- 1 /2 cup salad greens
- 2 teaspoon flax seed, powdered
- 1 teaspoon fresh dill, chopped

Dressing:

- 2 tablespoons apple cider vinegar
- 2 teaspoon olive oil
- salt and pepper per taste

Method:

1. Whisk together the ingredients of the dressing.

2. Construct the jar as follows:
   Bottom layer– brown rice
   Next layer – yellow pepper
   Next layer – zucchini
   Next layer – red pepper
   Next layer – salad greens
   Next layer – carrots
   Next layer – cashew
   Next layer – dill
   Last layer – flax seeds

3. Tightly screw the lid on to the jar. Refrigerate

4. Can last up to 3 days.

Roasted Sweet Potato with Quinoa

Serves 4

Ingredients:

- 4 medium sized sweet potatoes, roasted and diced into bite size pieces
- 2 cups quinoa, cooked
- 1 cup black beans, cooked or canned
- 1 red pepper, diced
- 4 cups salad greens of your choice
- 4 tablespoons cranberry, dried
- 4 tablespoons sunflower seeds, salted
- Salt and pepper to taste

Dressing:

- 1 cup mango, fresh or frozen, pureed
- 4 tablespoons balsamic vinegar
- 6 tablespoons water

Method:

1. For the dressing mix together pureed mango, vinegar and water

2. Construct the jars as follows:
   Bottom layer – black beans
   Next layer – quinoa
   Next layer – dressing
   Next layer – red pepper
   Next layer –greens
   Next layer – sweet potatoes
   Next layer –dried cranberries
   Last layer –sunflower seeds

3. Tightly screw the lids. Refrigerate.

4. Toss before eating.

5. Lasts up to 3 days.

Shrimp, Bacon and Feta Cheese delight

Serves 2

Ingredients:

- 15-16 shrimps, cooked
- 4 slices bacon
- 4 tablespoons feta cheese, chopped
- ½ cup corn
- 2 eggs, boiled, chopped into small pieces
- 4 tablespoons avocado, chopped
- 4 tablespoons cucumber, chopped
- 2 tablespoons red onion, chopped
- 16 cherry tomatoes
- A handful of romaine lettuce
- A handful of spinach
- Dressing of your choice (mentioned in above recipes)

Method:

1. Construct the jar as follows:
   Bottom layer – dressing
   Next layer – avocado
   Next layer – tomatoes
   Next layer – corn

Next layer – red onion
   Next layer – cucumber
   Next layer – lettuce
   Next layer – egg
   Next layer – spinach
   Next layer – shrimp
   Next layer – feta cheese
   Last layer – bacon

2. Tightly screw the lid. Refrigerate.

3. Can store up to 3 days

Californian rolls in a jar

Serves 2

Ingredients:

- 2 cups brown rice/ white rice, cooked
- 2 avocados, deseeded, remove skin and diced
- ½ tablespoon rice vinegar
- ½ teaspoon sugar
- ½ teaspoon soy sauce
- 1 tablespoon lemon juice
- 1 cucumber, peeled, deseeded, cut into thin matchstick size pieces
- 2 whole Nori sheets, cut into small pieces
- ½ cup lump crab meat

Method:

1. Heat vinegar and sugar in a saucepan until sugar is dissolved.
2. Pour over the rice when the rice is still warm. Add the soy sauce too. Toss.
3. Leave aside to cool to room temperature.
4. Meanwhile, brush lemon juice to the avocado.

5. Layer the mason jars as follows:
   Bottom layer- rice:
   Next layer – cucumber
   Next layer – Nori sheet
   Next layer – crab
   Top layer – avocado

6. Tightly screw the lids on the jar. Refrigerate.

7. Serve tossed.

Pepperoni Spaghetti

Serves 6

Ingredients:

- 1 ½ cups broken or cut spaghetti , boiled according to instructions
- 3 eggs
- 1 pound ricotta
- ½ package pepperoni, sliced
- ½ cup parmesan cheese, shredded
- Salt and pepper to taste.

Method:

1. Mix the spaghetti and ricotta.
2. Beat the eggs along with salt and pepper.
3. Fold the egg mixture into the spaghetti ricotta mixture.
4. Add the pepperoni and parmesan cheese.
5. Grease the mason jars.
6. Fill up the jars with the spaghetti mixture.
7. Bake at 350 degrees for 30-40 minutes.

Mason Jar Chicken Cordon Bleu

Serves 8

Ingredients:

- 1 1/ cups Plain Panko bread crumbs
- 1 tablespoon parsley flakes
- ½ teaspoon black pepper
- 1 teaspoon Kosher salt
- ½ cup melted butter, unsalted
- 10 slices Swiss cheese, about 10 ounces
- 9 slices smoked ham, 8 ounces
- ½ teaspoon black pepper
- 6 Chicken breast cutlets, 1 ¾ pounds

Method:

1. Onto a piece of plastic wrap, layer 6 chicken cutlets, touching and overlapping a bit. Similarly, use 3 chicken breasts and fillet each into 2 cutlets. Use a plastic wrap to cover the chicken.

2. Pound meat into a big sheet of chicken using a meat tenderizer and then sprinkle about a teaspoon of salt and black pepper, cracked. Use the smoked ham pieces to cover the chicken, and then top using 10 slices of Swiss cheese. Start to roll the chicken with the plastic wrap, working from the furthest side towards you.

3. Cut the chicken into 8 equal slices that are about 1 ½ -1 ¾ inches in thickness. Into a greased 8 ounce wide-mouth Mason jar, put the spirals and then add in panko Bread crumbs, parsley flakes, black pepper, melted butter and kosher salt.

4. Into 8 Mason jars, sub-divide the crumbs to about 3 tablespoons each. Then put the jars onto a cookie sheet and bake for 40 minutes at 375 degrees F. Tent the jars using foil 20 minutes into baking, to prevent the crumbs from burning. In about 5 minutes towards end-time, remove the foil.

5. Remove from oven and then serve, or cool on a wire rack. Cover and refrigerate until ready to serve, to facilitate freezing. Reheat by placing onto the microwave for 2 minutes uncovered.

Rice and Bean Burrito

Serves 4

Ingredients:

- 1 head butter lettuce, shredded
- 2 large red or yellow peppers, diced
- 1 cup canned corn or 2 fresh cobbs
- 1 tablespoon maple syrup
- ½ teaspoon salt
- 2 teaspoons chili powder
- 2 teaspoons cumin
- 2 tablespoons fresh lime juice
- 2 cups canned lentils, rinsed and drained
- 2 cups cooked brown rice

Method:

1. Start by preparing 2 cups of brown rice based on the package instructions. Once cooked, allow to chill.
2. Now whisk together chili powder, cumin, lime juice, olive oil, salt and maple syrup together. Over the dressing, pour your lentils and combine well. Subdivide the two cups of rice into 4 Mason jars, and then add in a layer of lentils to the jars.

3. Top the jars with lettuce, peppers and corn. You may also use cooked ground beef or shredded chicken for the recipe, and other veggies. Enjoy.

Mason Jar Stromboli

Serves 12

Ingredients:

- 1 teaspoon kosher salt
- 2 ½ cups All purpose flour
- 1 cup warm water
- 1teaspoon sugar
- 2 tablespoon yeast
- Parmesan cheese for sprinkling
- Italian Seasoning for sprinkling
- Garlic Salt for sprinkling
- 18 slices Genoa Salami
- 12 Provolone Cheese slices

Method:

1. Combine sugar and yeast in a large bowl and then pour some warm water over the yeast. Allow the yeast to set for 2 minutes before stirring salt and flour.

2. Knead the mixture until you get a soft dough ball. Add some more flour pinches in case the dough is very sticky. Roll out the dough into a big rectangle on a large and floured surface. The dough should be about ¼ inch thick. Then lay 2 rows of cheese.

3. Make three rows of salami, and sprinkle some parmesan cheese, Italian seasoning, and garlic salt. Now roll the dough from the end that is farthest from you, towards you making sure that you make a firm roll. Then pitch the seam closed.

4. Cut your Stromboli into 12 rolls using a sharp knife and put them into wide mouth mason jars (8-ounce) that are greased.

5. Into a preheated oven at 375 degrees, bake the rolls for 25-30 minutes, to have them turn golden brown and well cooked through. Allow to cool and then store in your fridge until ready to serve.

6. To serve, heat the jar in your microwave when uncovered for about 30 seconds until you obtain the temperature you need. Serve together with a little jar of marinara sauce. Alternatively, you can use pizza dough for the recipe ensuring to cut the slices to 1.5 inches.

Chicken Curry with Cilantro Rice

Serves 6

Ingredients:

- 1 lime cut into 6 wedges
- ¼ cup cilantro leaves, rough chopped
- Juice and zest of 1 lime
- 1 teaspoon kosher salt
- 3 cups water
- 1 ½ cups basmati rice rinsed and drained
- ½ cup sour cream
- 1-2 tablespoons curry powder
- 16-ounces jarred salsa
- 1 1/5-2 pounds chicken thighs, boneless and skinless

Method:

1. Cook the chicken, curry and salsa in a large skillet that is fitted with a lid. Under low heat, simmer the mixture for about 30 minutes. Then remove from heat and stir the sour cream.

2. Shred the chicken using 2 forks, and put it in 6 wide-mouth mason jars. Allow the rice, water, and salt to boil, and then lower the heat.

3. Simmer the rice, covered until tender, and the water is fully absorbed. Use a fork to fluff gently and then add some zest and juice from one lime, as well as cilantro. Continue to fluff for the cilantro and lime to incorporate.

4. Over the thick mixture, put about ¾ cup rice and then top with lime wedge, and chill completely, then cover. Put into your fridge for not more than 5 days as the sour cream might "break" if stored longer.

5. To serve, uncover the jar and remove the lime wedge, then put into the microwave for about 1 ½ minutes. When the jar is hot enough, turn it to remove the contents. You can sprinkle with lime juice and enjoy.

Chapter 4:
Soups in a Jar

Tortilla Soup

Serves 2

Ingredients:

- 1 ½ cups chicken broth
- 8 ounce red salsa
- 1 cup chicken, shredded, grilled
- ½ cup corn
- ½ cup black beans, canned, drained, rinsed
- ¼ teaspoon vegetable oil
- 2 corn tortillas
- ½ ripe avocado, diced
- 1 ½ tablespoons fresh cilantro, chopped finely

Method:

1. Heat the chicken broth and red salsa on a medium flame.
2. Once it starts boiling, add the chicken, corn and black beans.
3. Cook for 5-6 minutes.
4. Meanwhile, add the oil in a nonstick pan.

5. Add tortilla and cook on both the sides until crisp.
6. Cut the tortilla into strips.
7. Pour the soup into the mason jars.
8. Garnish with avocado, tortilla strips and cilantro.
9. Tightly screw on the lids. Refrigerate.
10. Serve heated.

Vegetable Soup

Serves 3

Ingredients:

- 4 cups tomatoes, chopped
- 3 cups potatoes, cubed
- 3 cups carrots, sliced into 3/4the inch pieces
- 2 cups lima beans
- 2 cups corn, uncooked
- 1 cup celery, sliced into 1 inch pieces
- 1 cup onions, chopped
- 3 cups water
- Salt and pepper to taste

Method:

1. Mix in all the vegetables along with water in a large bowl.
2. Bring to a boil. When it starts boiling, simmer it for 5 minutes
3. Season with salt and pepper then set it down to cool.
4. Store in mason jars. Refrigerate.
5. Reheat before serving.

Chicken Noodle Soup

Serves 3

Ingredients:

- 3 cups Chicken stock
- 1 ½ cup carrots, chopped sliced or chopped into the desired size
- 1 ½ cups celery sliced into the desired size
- 1 medium sized onion, chopped
- 1 cup egg noodles, cook according to instructions on the package. Keep the noodles slightly undercooked
- 1 cup chicken breast, chopped into small pieces
- Salt and pepper to taste
- 1 tablespoon Garlic powder
- Seasoning of your choice

Method:

1. In a large, pour in 5-6 cups of water.
2. Put in the chicken pieces and boil until cooked.
3. Add carrots and celery, boil for 5 more minutes.
4. Add the onions, salt, pepper and garlic powder.
5. Simmer until the onions are cooked.

6. Add the noodles and seasoning.

7. Simmer for another 15 minutes.

8. Cool and pour in mason jars.

9. Tightly screw on the lids. Refrigerate.

10. Reheat before serving.

Pasta Soup

Serves 4

Ingredients:

- 2 Cups pasta, parboiled
- ½ cup broccoli broken into smaller pieces
- ½ cup carrots, chopped into bite size pieces
- ½ cup each yellow, red and green bell pepper
- ½ cup shallots, chopped
- 1 tablespoon garlic, minced
- 1 teaspoon olive oil
- 2 tablespoons parsley, chopped
- ½ tablespoon oregano powder
- ½ tablespoon garlic powder
- Salt and pepper to taste
- 4 cups vegetable stock or water

Method:

1. In a large pan, put in the olive oil.
2. Add shallots and garlic, sauté for 1-2 minutes
3. Add all the other ingredients.

4. Bring to boil. Simmer for 15 minutes.
5. Set it down to cool.
6. Transfer into mason jars.
7. Tightly screw on the lids. Refrigerate.
8. Reheat before serving.

Instant Noodle Soup in a Jar

Serves 1

Ingredients:

- 12 leaves of baby spinach
- ½ cup shredded napa cabbage
- ½ cup shredded carrot
- ¼ teaspoon ginger, grated
- 1/8th teaspoon garlic powder
- ¼ of a stock cube
- ½ teaspoon lime juice
- 1 tablespoon soy sauce
- 1 ½ ounce rice noodle sticks

Method:

1. Obtain the rice noodles from the container, measure out 1 ½ ounces and then put into a zip lock bag. Break the noodles into little pieces by grabbing the zip lock bag with the hands and set aside.

2. To a 16-ounce mason jar, add in the remaining ingredients starting from the soy sauce, lime juice, stock cube, garlic powder, grated ginger, shredded carrots, napa cabbage and baby spinach.

3. Into the jar, pack the broken noodles and then screw the lid on and keep in the fridge for about 24 hours.

4. To serve, just pour boiling water into the jar, ensuring the water can cover the noodles, preferably 1 ½ cups. Now replace the lid and allow the noodles to soak until they turn soft, for about 12 minutes.

5. Gently mix the soup to allow the stock cube to dissolve. Use oven mitts or a towel to handle the jar as it will be very hot. To avoid cracking the glass jar, leave it to cool under room temperature for 15 minutes and then add the hot water. To serve, just tip into a bowl.

Beef Barley Soup Mix in a Jar

Serves 8

Ingredients:

- ¼ teaspoon dried garlic, minced
- ¼ teaspoon black pepper
- 2 bay leaves
- ½ teaspoon thyme leaves, dried
- 2 tablespoons celery flakes, dried
- ¼ cup instant beef bouillon
- ¼ cup dried onions, minced
- 2 tablespoons parsley flakes, dried
- ½ cup dried lentils
- 3/4 cup medium pearl barley, separated

For Beef Barley Soup:

- 10 cups water
- 1 tablespoon vegetable oil
- 2 pound lean hamburger or 2 pound beef chuck, boneless, cut in 1/2-inch pieces
- Contents of jar

Method:

1. Into 1-pint mason jar, layer the soup kit ingredients starting with half of pearl barley, dried lentils, parsley flakes, dried onions, beef bouillon, celery flakes, thyme leaves, bay leaves, black pepper and dried garlic. Put the remaining half of the barley on top and then firmly seal the jar with a lid. Keep the jar under refrigeration until needed.

2. To prepare the beef barley soap, heat some oil in a Dutch oven over medium heat. Now brown the meat and then pour off the drippings.

3. Open the Mason jar and pour the soup kit jar into the Dutch oven, bringing to a boil. Minimize the heat to low, cover and then simmer for about 1 ½ -1 ¾ hours. When done, the beef should now be fork tender. Discard the bay leaves and serve.

Layered Dried Bean Soup Mix

Serves 10

Ingredients:

- ½ cup split green peas
- ½ cup small red beans
- ½ cup red lentils
- ½ cup black beans
- ½ cup split yellow peas
- ½ cup kidney beans

For Seasoning Mix:

- 4 tablespoons brown sugar
- ½ teaspoon celery seed
- ½ teaspoon garlic powder
- ½ teaspoon black pepper
- 1 teaspoon parsley flakes, dried
- 1 ½ teaspoons salt
- 2 teaspoons dried minced onion
- 2 teaspoons chicken bouillon granules
- 1 tablespoon sweet pepper flakes, dried

- 1 teaspoon Liquid Smoke, optional

For Dried Bean Mix:

- 2 (14 ½ ounce) cans tomatoes

Method:

1. Into a 24 ounce clear Mason jar, layer each type of bean starting with split green peas, then red beans, red lentils, black beans, split yellow peas and finally kidney beans. Seal the jar and store until needed.

2. To prepare the soup, rinse the beans and then put in a stockpot or Dutch oven. Over the beans, pour about 4 cups of boiling water and allow to soak completely, overnight.

3. Now drain the beans from the water and put into the stockpot. Add in about 6 cups of water and boil over high heat while covered. Set the heat to low and allow the beans to simmer for about 1 to 1 ½ hours. The beans should be somehow tender.

4. Add in the seasoning mix and tomatoes, and stir. Cover the mixture and allow to simmer over low for 30 minutes. Then uncover the beans and simmer for an additional 1 hour for the soup to thicken and the beans to get tender. Serve when warm.

Rainbow Bean Soup Mix

Serves 12

Ingredients:

- 3/4 cup dried black beans
- 3/4 cup lentils
- 3/4 cup dried split peas
- 3/4 cup dried great northern beans
- 3/4 cup dried red beans

For the seasoning:

- 1 teaspoon oregano, dried
- 1 teaspoon pepper
- 1 teaspoon garlic powder
- 1 1/2 teaspoons chili powder
- 2 teaspoons lemonade drink mix, sweetened
- 2 teaspoons dried basil
- 2 tablespoons parsley flakes, dried
- 2 tablespoons beef bouillon granules
- 2 tablespoons dried onion flakes, dried

Optional:

- 5-ounce canned ham can

Method:

1. Layer all the bean types in a quart-sized Mason jar starting with the red beans, followed by the northern beans, split beans, lentils and the black beans. Store refrigerated until you are ready to use.

2. To prepare the soup, first remove the seasoning from the jar and then rinse the beans. Into a large dish that is heatproof, put the rinsed beans and then cover with 1-2 inches of water on top of the beans. Use a plastic wrap to cover the dish lightly.

3. Over high heat, heat in a microwave for a while then rotate after about 7 minutes. Drain and rinse the beans well and transfer into a large pot. Add in about 8 cups of water, the seasonings and 15-ounces can of crushed tomatoes.

4. Cover the mixture and allow to boil gently. Set the heat to low and then simmer for 1 ½ hours when covered, until the beans get tender. Continue to stir until ready to serve.

Meat and Tomato Mix soup

Serves: 12

Ingredients:

- 1 (28-ounce) can diced tomatoes
- 6 cups water
- 6 cups low-sodium beef or chicken broth
- 1 pound lean ground beef or turkey

Ingredients for mix:

- ½ cup macaroni noodles
- ½ cup long-grain white rice
- 2 teaspoons Italian seasoning
- ¼ cup dry, minced onions
- ½ cup dry lentils
- ¼ cup pearl barley
- ½ cup dry split peas

Method:

1. Into a clean 1-quart mason jar, layer the white rice, Italian seasoning, minced onions, lentils, pearl barley, and split peas. Firmly close the jar and store until needed.

2. To make the soup, first brown the meat and drain it. Put into a large pot and add in tomatoes, water, and broth. Then open the Mason jar and pour the contents into the mixture.

3. Allow the mixture to boil and then set the heat to low, to simmer for about 60 minutes. Now add in the macaroni and cook for 10-15 minutes, until set. Only add sufficient macaroni to the portion you are serving, to avoid having overcooked pasta in leftovers. Serve.

Holiday Split Pea Soup Mix

Serves 6

Ingredients:

- 1 bay leaf
- 1 ½ cups split green peas, dried
- 1 teaspoon parsley flakes, dried
- 2 teaspoons minced onion, dried
- 2 teaspoons of celery flakes
- 2 teaspoons of imitation bacon bits
- 1 tablespoon of chicken bouillon granules
- 2 ¾ ounce package of country gravy mix

Method:

1. Into a pint jar, pour the country gravy mix. Then stir together parsley flakes, onions, celery flakes, bacon bits, and bouillon granules.

2. Pour this mixture into the Mason jar to constitute the second layer. Then add in the peas, and the bay leaf before sealing. Store the jar in the fridge until needed.

3. To make the soup, pour the contents from the jar into a Dutch oven or sauced pan, and then add in 6 cups of water. Bring the mixture to a boil, and then set the heat to low.

4. Simmer for 1-1 ½ hours, ensuring that you stir regularly. When the peas get tender, remove the bay leaf, and serve. You can top with bacon bits and dollop of sour cream if preferred.

Chapter 5:
Desserts in a Mason Jar

Banana and cream

Serves 3

Ingredients:

- ½ box instant vanilla pudding, made according to the instructions
- 1 cup milk
- 1 cup cream cheese, softened
- ¼ cup sweetened condensed milk
- 2 cups whipped cream
- ¼ teaspoon vanilla extract
- 8-10 cookies, crushed coarsely
- 2-3 bananas, sliced

Method:

1. In a bowl, beat with an electric mixer the cream cheese, condensed milk and vanilla until smooth.
2. In another bowl, whisk the pudding and milk.
3. Mix the pudding mixture into the cream cheese mixture.
4. Add one cup of the whipped cream to it.

5. Construct the jars as follows:
   Bottom layer – cookies
   Next layer - a little of the pudding mixture
   Next layer – few slices of bananas
   Next layer – a little of the whipped cream
   Repeat the layers once. Sprinkle some cookie crumbs on the top.

6. Tightly screw on the lids. Refrigerate

7. While serving, garnish with some slices of banana.

Caramel Brownies

Serves 4

Ingredients:

- 4-5 brownies, chopped into ¾ inch pieces or crumbled
- 3 cups chocolate pudding, made according to instructions
- ¼ cup black coffee
- 2 cups whipped cream
- 2 chocolate bars (1.4 oz. each) crushed
- ¼ teaspoon salt

Method:

1. Construct the jars as follows:
   Bottom layer – brownies
   Next layer – sprinkle coffee
   Next layer – caramel sauce
   Next layer – sprinkle salt
   Next layer – chocolate pudding
   Next layer – whipped cream
   Repeat the layer once.
   Drizzle some caramel sauce and crushed chocolate to top

2. Tightly screw on the lids.

3. Refrigerate.

Fruit Parfait

Serves 2

Ingredients:

- ¼ cup bananas, sliced
- ¼ cup strawberries
- ¼ cup ripe mango, diced
- ½ cup berries of your choice
- ¼ cup apples, peeled, cored, diced
- 2 slices cake, crumbled
- 4 tablespoons walnuts chopped
- 2 tablespoons fresh cream
- 2 tablespoons orange juice
- chocolate sauce to drizzle
- Strawberry sauce to drizzle

Method:

1. Mix together all the fruits in a bowl.
2. Construct the jars as follows:
   Bottom layer – cake
   Next layer – sprinkle orange juice
   Next layer – fresh cream
   Next layer – fruits

Next layer – walnuts
Next layer – drizzle the chocolate sauce and strawberry sauce
Repeat the layer

3. Tightly screw the lid on the jars.

4. Refrigerate.

Blueberry Cheesecake

Serves 6

Ingredients:

- 6 whole graham crackers, crushed
- ¼ cup sugar
- 2 tablespoons butter, melted
- ¼ teaspoon cinnamon powder

For the Cheesecake:

- 1 ½ cup cream cheese softened
- ½ cup sweetened condensed milk
- ¼ cup sugar
- 2 large eggs
- ½ tablespoon vanilla extract
- ¼ cup sour cream

Blueberry topping:

- ½ cup blueberry jam
- 1 cup fresh blueberries
- 1 tablespoon orange juice
- ¾ tablespoon cornstarch

- ½ teaspoon vanilla extract

Method:

1. In a bowl, mix together graham crackers. Sugar, butter and cinnamon powder.

2. Press it into the mason jars.

For the Cheesecake layer

1. Beat with an electric mixer the cream cheese and sugar until smooth and fluffy

2. Add the condensed milk, vanilla and sour cream. Beat for a minute.

3. Add the eggs one at a time and beat well. Further beat for 2 minutes until fluffy.

4. Divide the batter into the jars. Keep the jars in a baking pan.

5. Add water to fill ¾ of the pan

6. Bake at 350 degrees F for 30 minutes

7. Remove from oven and cool until room temperature in the pan.

Blueberry topping

1. In a microwave safe bowl, mix together blueberry jam, 1/2 the blueberries, cornstarch and orange juice.

2. Microwave on high for 5 minutes stirring in between

3. Remove from microwave and mix in the remaining blueberries and vanilla extract.

4. Crush the berries with the back of the spoon.

5. Leave aside to cool.

6. Pour the topping in the jars.

7. Tightly screw the lid of the jars.

8. Refrigerate.

9. Stores up to 3 days.

Butterfinger pies in a jar

Serves 4

Ingredients:

Graham cracker crust

- 12 whole graham crackers, powdered coarsely
- 2 tablespoons brown sugar
- 6 tablespoons melted butter,

Peanut butter layer

- 2 cups cream cheese, softened
- 2 cups sugar, powdered. Sifted
- 4 tablespoons brown sugar
- 1 cup peanut butter (creamy)
- 1 teaspoon vanilla extract
- 1 ½ cup chilled whipping cream
- 2 regular sized butter finger candy bar, finely chopped

Method:

1. For the Graham cracker crust: Mix together all the ingredients.
2. Press this crust into Mason jars. Place the jars on a baking sheet.

3. Bake in a preheated oven at 350 F for 6-8 minutes. Keep aside to cool.

4. For the peanut butter layer: Whip chilled cream with powdered sugar until stiff peaks are formed.

5. In another bowl, beat cream cheese until smooth.

6. Brown sugar. Beat again.

7. Mix peanut butter and vanilla. Add 2 cups of the whipped cream to it

8. Mix briefly at a low speed. Using a rubber spatula fold the mixture.

9. Refrigerate the remaining whipped cream.

10. Layer the crust filled mason jars as follows:
Above the crust – butter finger candy bar
Next – divide the filling among the jars

11. Tightly screw on the lids. Refrigerate.

12. Serve with whipped cream on top.

Buttermilk Panna Cotta

Serves: 6

Ingredients:

- 1½ cups of whipping cream
- 2¼ teaspoons of gelatine
- ⅓ cup of sugar
- ¼ cup of sour cream
- 1¼ cups of buttermilk

Method:

1. Into a small sauce pan, pour the butter milk and then sprinkle the gelatine on top. Allow to chill for about 2 minutes, to have the gelatin grains begin to swell.

2. Over low heat, stir in the sugar and then gently heat until the gelatin and the sugar dissolve fully, but do not boil.

3. Remove the mixture from heat and then whisk in the sour cream as well as the whipping cream. Put under refrigeration for about 30 minutes, or chill until it's safe to touch.

4. After cooling, now whisk the panna cotta for another time before pouring into little Mason jars. Cover and then refrigerate for about 4 hours, until set.

Molten orange chocolate lava cakes

Serves 6

Ingredients:

- 4 eggs
- ¼ teaspoon salt
- 3 tablespoons flour
- 1/3 cup sugar, granulated
- 1 tablespoon orange zest
- 1 tablespoon Grand Marnier
- 8 ounces dark chocolate
- 7 tablespoons butter, unsalted

Method:

1. Butter the insides and the bottom of a 6-ounce Mason jar using a tablespoon of butter. Melt chocolate and butter together into a double boiler that is over simmering water. When melted, remove from heat and then stir in the orange zest Grand Marnier.

2. Sift in some salt, flour, and sugar and stir to mix. Beat in the eggs using an electric beater, one at a time for 3 minutes. When done, the chocolate should be lightly a light shade of brown in color.

3. Pour about 1/3 cup of batter into each mason jars and put into the fridge for 20 minutes, or overnight.

4. Preheat your oven to about 400 degrees F and take out the jars from the fridge. Put the jars on a baking sheet and then bake until the top is set in the center, for 8-10 minutes. When done, remove from heat and chill for some time. Dust using powdered sugar, if needed. Serve the cake when warm.

Creme Caramel

Serves: 6

Ingredients:

- 1 teaspoons Tahitian vanilla
- ½ cup sugar
- 4 egg yolks
- 1 cup heavy cream
- 1 cup milk
- 1/3 cup water
- 2/3 cup sugar

Method:

1. Preheat your oven to about 325 degrees F.

2. In a saucepan, put sugar and then heat over low heat, to allow the sugar to dissolve. Set the heat to high and boil the sugar to have it turn golden brown, and then remove from heat.

3. Pour the hot caramel very fast into six 4-ounce jars, and allow to chill for some time. Scald the cream and milk into a separate pan until bubbles form, but should not boil.

4. Combine vanilla, sugar and egg yolks until it's smooth and fully blended, without allowing air into the mixture. Whisk some tablespoons of the hot milk mixture

carefully into the egg to temper it. Then whisk again in the rest of the hot milk.

5. Using a strainer, transfer the mixture into a clean bowl, to catch egg clumps that may have been formed. Into the bottom of a 13x9 inch baking pan, lay a tea towel and then put the Mason jars on the towel.

6. Into each of the jars, pour the custard mixture and then add in boiling water. The water should be somehow halfway up the jars, taking caution not to have the water enter the custard.

7. Use an aluminum foil to cover a 13x9 inch pan, and then bake in a preheated oven at 325 degrees F. After about 35 minutes, your custards should almost be set.

8. Remove the custards from the water very carefully, and allow them to chill for around 10 minutes. Now cover and keep into the fridge for about 3 hours, until completely chilled.

9. Use a cup to serve the crème caramel, or dip into hot water. Then run a knife around each of the side, and invert the custard into a plate.

Salted Caramel Brownie Trifles

Serves: 8

Ingredients:

- 8 jelly-size mason jars
- 3 (1.4 ounces) Heath chocolate toffee bars, crushed
- 1 (8 ounces) carton frozen whipped topping, thawed
- 6 snack cups chocolate pudding, prepared
- Coarse sea salt
- 1 jar caramel sauce
- ¼ cup coffee, room temperature
- 1 box fudge brownie mix, & ingredients needed on the box

Method:

1. Follow the package directions to prepare the brownie batter, where you can substitute the coffee for water as needed on the fudge box.

2. Into a preheated oven, bake the batter at 350 degrees F for 20-25 minutes, in a greased pan. Once done, insert a tooth pick into the center to test whether it comes out clean, then remove to a wire rack and slice into ¾ inch sizes.

3. Make the trifles by putting little pieces of cooled brownie into the bottom of 8 jelly-size mason jars. Try

to break the brownie into smaller piece in order to fit into the jar. Then drizzle caramel sauce over the brownies and sprinkle some salt.

4. To the jar, add in a chocolate pudding layer, followed by a layer of whipped topping, and then sprinkle the crushed health bar to each trifle. Do the same for the other mason jars, and finish using the whipped topping.

5. Then drizzle caramel sauce onto each trifle and a crushed health bar sprinkle. Store the jars in the fridge until serving time.

Banana Split Parfait

Serves 3

Ingredients:

For whipped cream:

- ½ teaspoon corn flour
- 1 teaspoon of vanilla extract or ½ teaspoon vanilla bean paste
- 1 cup heavy whipping cream (36%-40% milk fat)

For Chocolate Sauce:

- A little Vanilla paste or vanilla extract
- 2 teaspoons powdered sugar
- 4 teaspoons milk
- 3 teaspoons cocoa powder

For Layers:

- ½ cup crushed walnuts
- 1 cup sliced bananas
- 1 cup sliced strawberries

Method:

1. Whip sugarless whipping vanilla cream and keep in the fridge until ready to use. Combine milk and cocoa powder in a small bowl and blend with a spoon to smoothness. Then add in powdered sugar and vanilla paste and mix until smooth.

2. Layer in mason jar starting with the whipped cream, then the chocolate sauce, walnuts, strawberries and the bananas. Also, include other ingredients you'd like such as pineapples.

Chapter 6:
Smoothies in a Jar

Fruity Green tea smoothie

Serves 2

Ingredients:

- ½ cup green tea
- 1 cup yogurt
- ½ cup fresh berries (blueberries, raspberries or black berries)

Variations: Replace the berries with bananas, or kiwi, or mangoes

Method:

1. Blend together the green tea, yogurt and the fresh berries.
2. Pour in mason jars.
3. Tightly screw on the lid. Refrigerate.
4. Serve with crushed ice.

Banana Smoothie

Serves 2

Ingredients:

- 2 bananas, sliced
- 2 cups almond milk , unsweetened
- 1 teaspoon maple syrup
- 1 teaspoon cinnamon powder

Method:

1. Blend with an electric mixer bananas, almond milk, maple syrup and three fourth of the cinnamon powder.
2. Pour in the mason jars.
3. Sprinkle with the remaining cinnamon.
4. Tightly screw on the lids.
5. Refrigerate.

Strawberry Almond Butter Smoothie

Serves 3

Ingredients:

- 3 cups milk or almond milk
- 3 tablespoons chia seeds
- ¾ cup rolled oats
- 2 tablespoons almond butter
- 3 tablespoons honey
- 4 cups fresh or frozen strawberries

Method:

1. Blend all the ingredients with an electric mixer until smooth
2. Pour into mason jars.
3. Screw on the lid tightly. Refrigerate
4. Can store up to 2 days

Mango Smoothie

Serves 3

Ingredients:

- ¾ cup ripe mango, chopped
- ¾ cup ripe avocado, mashed
- 1 ½ cups mango juice
- ¾ cup yogurt
- 3 tablespoons sugar

Method:

1. Blend all the ingredients with an electric mixer.
2. Pour into mason jars.
3. Screw the lids on tightly. Refrigerate.
4. Serve with ice cubes.
5. Can store up to 3 days.

Banana and Peanut Butter Smoothie

Serves 3

Ingredients:

- 1 ½ cup milk
- 1 ½ cup yogurt
- 6 tablespoons peanut butter, unsalted
- 1 Banana
- 3 tablespoons honey

Method:

1. Blend all the ingredients with an electric mixer.
2. Pour into mason jars.
3. Tightly screw on the lids. Refrigerate
4. Serve with ice cubes.
5. Can store up to 2 days.

Strawberry Oatmeal Smoothie

Serves 2

Ingredients:

- ½ cup rolled oats
- 3 teaspoons chia seeds
- 2 cups almond milk or plain milk
- ½ cup yogurt, low fat
- 2 cups strawberries, chopped
- 2 tablespoons pecan meal/ nut butter
- ½ teaspoon cinnamon, powdered
- 1 teaspoon vanilla extract
- 2 scoops vanilla protein powder (optional)
- Honey to taste

Method:

1. In a blender, add the chia seeds and oats. Blend until a fine powder.
2. Add rest of the ingredients and blend until smooth.
3. Pour into mason jars.
4. Tightly screw on the lids. Refrigerate.
5. Serve chilled.

Quick & Easy Mason Jar Smoothie

Serves 3

Ingredients:

- 1 cup vanilla yogurt, nonfat
- ½ cup peaches and juice, canned
- 1 cup frozen strawberries, unsweetened

Method:

1. Into a blender, put a cup of frozen strawberries, canned peaches and juice, and non-fat vanilla yoghurt. Blend until smooth.

2. Pour the smoothie into a pint-size Mason jar and refrigerate. To serve, thaw for a minute in a microwave on high and then stir.

Make Ahead Smoothies

Serves 2-3

Ingredients:

- 1 handful spinach
- 1 cup frozen berries
- 1 tablespoon chia seeds
- 1 scoop protein powder
- 1 cup almond milk

Method:

1. Into a blender, add a handful of spinach, frozen berries, chia seeds, protein powder, and almond milk.
2. Pour the smoothie into 2-cup mason jars, but leave a space at the top since accumulation of gases may break your jar.
3. Refrigerate the mason jar, until you're ready for serving.

Chapter 7:
Beverages in a Mason Jar

White Chocolate Latte

Serves 6

Ingredients:

- 4 cups milk
- 2 cups half and half (half milk and half cream)
- 1 ½ cup white chocolate pieces
- 4 tablespoons instant coffee
- 2 teaspoons vanilla extract
- ½ teaspoon almond extract
- Garnish with cinnamon sticks and whipped cream

Method:

1. In a saucepan add milk, half and half, white chocolate and instant coffee
2. Heat it on a low flame until all the chocolate is melted.
3. Add vanilla extract and almond extract. Mix well. Cool.
4. Pour into mason jars.
5. Tightly screw on the lids. Refrigerate.
6. Serve with ice, whipped cream and cinnamon sticks.
7. Can store up to 2 days.

Lemonade

Serves 4

Ingredients:

- ¾ cup lemon juice, freshly squeezed
- ¼ cup sugar
- 3 cups water
- 1 cup fresh strawberries, stemmed and pureed
- ½ cup heavy cream
- Garnish with Lemon slices

Method:

1. In a container, add lemon juice, sugar and 1 cup of water.
2. Stir until the sugar is dissolved.
3. Add the remaining 2 cups of water, strawberry puree
4. Mix well.
5. Pour into mason jars.
6. Tightly screw on the lids. Refrigerate.
7. Serve with ice cubes, cream and lemon slices
8. Can store up to 2 days.

Fruit Delight

Serves 6

Ingredients:

- 1 ½ cups fresh or frozen lemonade
- 1 ½ cups light rim
- 5 cups frozen or fresh fruit
- Sugar or sweetener (optional) to taste
- Garnish with a little fresh fruit

Variations: The fruits you can use

- Strawberries
- Blueberries
- Mango
- Peach
- Pineapple (add 1 cup canned coconut milk for pina colada)

Method:

1. Blend with an electric mixer lemonade, rum and fruit until smooth.
2. Pour into mason jars.
3. Tightly screw on the lids.

4. Freeze it.

5. Remove it at least an hour before serving. It should be in a slushy state.

Coffee in a jar

Serves 4

Ingredients:

- 2 cup milk
- 2 cups blended strong coffee
- 5 tablespoons brown sugar
- ½ teaspoon cinnamon powder

Method:

1. Blend all the ingredients with an electric mixer.
2. Pour in mason jars
3. Tightly screw the lids.
4. Refrigerate
5. Serve with ice cubes.

Chocó-coffee delight

Serves 4

Ingredients:

- 2 cup espresso coffee
- 3 tablespoons chocolate syrup
- 2 tablespoons sweetened condensed milk
- 2 tablespoons dark chocolate shavings

Method:

1. Blend together in an electric mixer coffee, chocolate syrup, condensed milk until smooth.
2. Pour into mason jars.
3. Tightly screw the lids. Refrigerate
4. Serve with ice cubes and chocolate shavings.

Strawberry Milk

Serves 1

Ingredients:

- 1/3 cup instant milk powder, strawberry
- 3 ½ tablespoons of plain creamer, nondairy
- 3 tablespoons of sugar, powdered
- 1 tablespoon of dry milk powder, nonfat
- ¾ cup + 1 tablespoon dry milk powder, nonfat
- Mini marshmallows (optional)

Method:

1. Into a bowl, combine all the ingredients and then add ¾ cup of boiling water to make a 1/3 cup serving size drink.

2. Stir completely and then top using the mini marshmallows. Transfer into a 16-ounce Mason jar and keep under refrigeration until ready to serve.

Hot spiced tea and cider mix

Serves 4

Ingredients:

- 1 teaspoon cloves
- 2 teaspoons cinnamon
- 2 cups sugar
- ½ cup instant iced tea mix
- 1 package lemonade mix, unsweetened
- 2 cups instant orange drink mix

Method:

1. Into a large bowl, mix together cloves, cinnamon, sugar, instant tea mix, lemonade mix and instant orange drink mix. When fully combined, pour into an airtight one-quart Mason jar, and seal the jar. Refrigerate the jar until ready for use.

2. To make a cup serving of hot spiced tea, just add a tablespoon of the mix, or more to your taste to a cup of hot water.

3. To prepare hot spiced cider, add 2/3 cup of the mix to ½ gallon of hot apple cider. Stir completely to dissolve.

Blueberry Infused Vodka Lemonade

Serves 2

Ingredients:

- ½ cup blueberries, frozen
- ½ cup blueberries, fresh
- Lemon slices for garnish
- Lemonade
- Vodka
- 1 teaspoon sugar

Method:

1. Into the bottom of a mason jar, put fresh blueberries and pour sufficient amount of vodka over the berries. Ensure that you fill the jar.

2. The vodka should turn cloudy and later become purple as it infuses. Allow the infusion to proceed for 12-36 hours and then strain the vodka. Preserve the berries for the garnish.

3. Thaw out frozen berries into a small bowl and combine with sugar. Pour the sugared berries into a separate mason jar or serving glass and add in a bunch of ice.

4. To serve, pour into a jar one part vodka and 2 parts lemonade and stir completely. To garnish, add in the berries soaked in vodka and a slice of lemon.

Iced Mocha

Serves 1-2

Ingredients:

- 1 cup milk, skim, 2% or whole
- 2 tablespoons sugar
- 2 tablespoons cocoa powder, Hershey's
- 1 (6-8 ounce) cup of strong, hot coffee
- Chocolate syrup
- Whipped cream
- Ice

Method:

1. Into a mason jar, combine sugar and cocoa powder completely, and then add in a cup of milk. Continue to stir until the contents are fully incorporated. Seal the jar and store in your fridge until ready to drink.

2. To serve, pour into a tall glass of ice and then use chocolate syrup and whipped cream as your topping, if desired.

Conclusion

Thank you for downloading this eBook. We sincerely hope you found it interesting and are excited to try these recipes for the upcoming holiday season.

In this eBook we have covered categories of Mason jar recipes: Salads, soups, breakfast, lunch, dinner, beverages, smoothies and desserts. This gives you a wide variety of recipes to choose from. Your gifting woes are taken care off now that you can create personalized gifts for your loved ones according to your choice.

We hope that the recipes provided in this eBook were helpful, easy to make and we also hope that you will refer to it again for your future needs.

Thank you and happing cooking!

Key Takeaways From This Book

1. Making mason jar meals is easy and convenient.

2. You can make mason jar meals in advance for breakfast, lunch, dinner, snacks, deserts and even drinks.

3. Mason jar meals encourage you to eat healthy even if you live a busy life.

4. Mason jar meals can be stored for long periods if properly stored.

5. They can be good gift ideas.

How To Put This Information Into Action

- First, you need to invest in some good jars that can withstand heat in case you want to prepare bake desserts.

- Once you have your jars, you can choose the various recipes you would want to try out.

- Always remember to clean your jars with hot water to sterilize the container adequately.

- In case you are putting some hot liquid in the jars, put the jars in some hot water to ensure that the jars do not break due to the sudden change in temperature.

- Once you fill your jars with the dessert, remember to wipe the rims to ensure that your jar is properly stored.

RESOURCES FOR FURTHER VIEWING AND READING

Websites:

28 Incredible Meals You Can Make in a Mason Jar
http://www.buzzfeed.com/candacelowry/incredible-meals-you-can-make-in-a-mason-jar

Mason Jar Recipes
https://www.pinterest.com/katlthomas/mason-jar-recipes/

Big Red Kitchen Mason Jar Meals
http://www.bigredkitchen.com/recipes/mason-jar-meals/

PREVIEW OF HYDROGEN PEROXIDE HANDBOOK

Chapter 2.
Health Benefits of Hydrogen Peroxide

Effects on health

Food grade hydrogen peroxide is a specially purified and refined form of hydrogen peroxide that is completely safe for consumption. In fact, the hydrogen peroxide easily available in drug stores and meant for application on external wounds and infections is not in any way dangerous for internal consumption. Hydrogen peroxide is an exceptionally powerful antimicrobial, especially when it comes to bacteria, and it has the ability to oxidize a wide range of unwanted substances. There are numerous uncontested health benefits associated with hydrogen peroxide, while there are others whose status is somewhat controversial.

Health Applications of hydrogen peroxide

Remedies

Hydrogen peroxide can be used in singlet oxygen therapy because it can release a single oxygen atom upon contact with other elements in an oxidation reaction. After the release of the oxygen atom, the remainder of the hydrogen peroxide molecule disintegrates and breaks down to form water. The single oxygen atom that is released into the body is very reactive and can oxidize or reduce the molecular structure of any undesirable organisms or compounds present in the body – for instance, parasites, fungi, bacteria, and foreign proteins. It can also oxidize or reduce any tissue that has been affected by disease or infection. This atomic oxygen, O_1, has a very high energy and an enhanced capacity for healing as compared to the atmospheric oxygen, O_2, which humans normally breathe.

First Aid and External Contamination

Hydrogen peroxide is probably most popular for its strong capabilities in disinfecting minor cuts and treating minor infections. Standard food grade concentrations are safe for such external application, despite the fact that they are often sold in rather higher concentrations than drug store hydrogen peroxide. For instance, conventional drug store hydrogen peroxide is diluted to about 3.5 percent, whereas food grade offerings have a range of between 8 to 35 percent. Food grade hydrogen peroxide is thus likely to cause a slight tingling or burning sensation upon application to an open wound. However, this does not mean that it will cause severe damage, or indeed any damage whatsoever, to healthy, functioning tissue. According to *Biochemical, Physiological, and Molecular Aspects of Human Nutrition* by Dr. Martha H. Stipanuk, hydrogen peroxide has the ability to damage and destroy virtually all harmful pathogens upon contact.

Oral Health and Nourishment

Food grade hydrogen peroxide has a very significant effect on your teeth. It is not harmful and does not have to be diluted to a lower concentration; there is absolutely no need to be afraid of using it. It may lead to a rather intense tingling or burning sensation, but also to a potent effect on harmful oral bacteria! In any case, a hydrogen peroxide concentration of 3.5% is all that is really required to put down your oral pathogens. This means you can save money by diluting a sufficient amount of the food grade hydrogen peroxide for daily oral use. A range of proven health benefits are associated with oral use of hydrogen peroxide, including teeth whitening, reduced risk of gum disease, fewer canker sores and cavities, and most obviously, fresher breath.

Detoxification using hydrogen peroxide

The human body system has the ability to get rid of toxins with the help of four critical organs: the lungs, the kidneys, the skin, and the colon (aided by the liver). A bath of hydrogen peroxide can assist in the cleansing and purification of the skin. This hydrogen peroxide bath helps destroy organisms and toxins, and even reduces the residues that are left after the use of soap.

One of the best things about hydrogen peroxide is that it performs its detoxification function in an environmentally friendly manner: the only byproducts released are oxygen and water. All you need for a hydrogen peroxide bath is a bathtub and two quarts of hydrogen peroxide.

Directions for hydrogen peroxide bath therapy

1. Pour a single quart of hydrogen peroxide into a hot bath. Make sure that you mix it thoroughly to avoid any sort of skin irritation.

2. You should be very careful not to get any water in your eyes, as it might lead to irritation.

3. Fully immerse yourself in the water and then wait for about five minutes.

4. If there is absolutely no noticeable reaction on your skin, you need to add the second quart and stir thoroughly again. Relax and soak for about twenty to twenty-five minutes.

5. The residue that is left behind after a thorough skin detoxification bath will definitely amaze you!

6. Brushing dry skin all over your body will boost the efficacy of the bath.

Brushing the dry skin gets rid of the layer of dead skin that can be a hindrance to absorption of both nutrients and energy from the bath. The brushing of dry skin also stimulates the lymph fluids and the blood to rise to the skin surface, which the skin to accommodate the healing effects of the hydrogen peroxide bath. For detoxification therapy, take this bath for a minimum of seven successive days, or as recommended by a medical practitioner. However, weekly or even monthly treatments can have a very beneficial effect on your skin nutrition.

Disease Prevention

The antibacterial qualities of hydrogen peroxide make it very suitable for many uses in the improvement of the heath of the human body. Hydrogen peroxide has the ability to fight bacteria, yeast, viruses, and parasites. In fact, quite a number of healthcare professionals have used these advantageous properties of hydrogen peroxide to aid internal parts of the body, for instance the immune system. Medical practitioners have tangible evidence that hydrogen peroxide therapy treatments can have significant positive effects on medical conditions such as human papilloma virus, asthma, degenerative spinal disc disease, leukemia, multiple sclerosis, and arthritis.

The main reason why hydrogen peroxide is applied in the prevention of diseases is the knowledge that infected cells and harmful microorganisms cannot survive in environments that are very rich in oxygen. Since hydrogen peroxide emits oxygen upon its disintegration, once consumed, it is a very efficient supply of oxygen for the internal body systems. This enables the strengthening of the immune system, thereby helping in prevention of diseases and infections.

To treat certain specific infections and prevent them from accelerating, hydrogen peroxide can be consumed in a variety of ways as part of medical hydrogen peroxide therapy. Medical practitioners may suggest its administration either orally or through intravenous injections. Oral administration is simply done by diluting a certain proportion of hydrogen peroxide with water and drinking it.

To prevent diseases at home, you can ensure that all your surfaces are thoroughly cleaned using diluted hydrogen peroxide to get rid of any contamination that might lead to infections. Food-grade hydrogen peroxide can be used to thoroughly clean grocery purchases such as vegetables and fruits. Contaminated vegetables and fruits can lead to chronic stomach upsets if they are not thoroughly disinfected before consumption.

Hydrogen peroxide is also useful in simple health practices – for instance, in the care of your ears to prevent infections, you can use a drop of diluted hydrogen peroxide as a means of softening earwax so you can get rid of any painful or irritating lumps.

Hydrogen peroxide not only offers health benefits to the human body but also presents very real advantages in plant health. If your plants consistently suffer from root rot, hydrogen peroxide is a great remedy. Just apply a solution of thirty parts water to one part hydrogen peroxide at the base of your plants to effectively end the problem. This also encourages root nourishment and development of strong and healthy root systems. Keep applying hydrogen peroxide in this manner to avoid future encounters with root rot.

To download the rest of this book, please click on the following link:

http://www.amazon.com/Hydrogen-Peroxide-Secrets-Optimum-Prevention-ebook/dp/B00NVN9IYM

Did You Like Mason Jar Meals Surprisingly Quick, Easy and Healthy Mason Jar Meal Recipe Ideas for People on the Go?

Before you leave, I wanted to say thank-you again for buying my book.

I know you could have picked from a number of different books on this topic, but you chose this one, so I can't thank you enough for doing that and reading until the end.

I'd like to ask you a small favor.

If you enjoyed this book or feel that it has helped you in anyway, then could you please take a minute and post an honest review about it on Amazon?

Your review will help get my book out there to more people and they'll be grateful, as will I.

More Books You Might Like

If the links do not work, for whatever reason, you can simply search for these titles on the Amazon website to find them.

Household DIY: Save Time and Money with Do It Yourself Hints and Tips on Furniture, Clothes, Pests, Stains, Residues, Odors and More!

DIY Household Hacks: Save Time and Money with Do It Yourself Tips and Tricks for Cleaning Your House

Essential Oils: Essential Oils & Aromatherapy for Beginners: Proven Secrets to Weight Loss, Skin Care, Hair Care & Stress Relief Using Essential Oil Recipes

Apple Cider Vinegar for Beginners: An Apple Cider Vinegar Handbook with Proven Secrets to Natural Weight Loss, Optimum Health and Beautiful Skin

Body Butter Recipes: Proven Formula Secrets to Making All Natural Body Butters that Will Hydrate and Rejuvenate Your Skin

If the links do not work, for whatever reason, you can simply search for these titles on the Amazon website to find them.

www.ingramcontent.com/pod-product-compliance
Lightning Source LLC
Chambersburg PA
CBHW071419070526
44578CB00003B/615